ISBN-13: 978-1

ISBN-10: 179

Copyright © 2009

TABLE OF CONTENTS

INTRODUCTION – WHAT IS VISUALIZAITON?

There is only one admirable form of the imagination: the imagination that is so intense that it creates a new reality, that it makes things happen.—Sean O'Faolain

As humans, we have the amazing ability to conjure pictures inside our heads. We can elicit pictures of past moments, as when we reminisce an old flame. We can generate pictures of future events, as when we plan a beach getaway. We can even invoke pictures of objects in our environment such as a new car or of non-existent things yet to be created, like a colorful painting.

This ability to see in our mind has provided us with many benefits. It allowed our prehistoric ancestors to stare at a rock and envision how it might look in the future—perhaps as a spear if chiseled in the right way. In modern times, it allows us to envision accomplishments much grander, like skyscrapers, and more complicated, like laptop computers.

There is a far more practical use for this talent, however, which many people don't realize. Creating visions within your mind, in the form of visualization, can help you create changes in yourself and in your life. I'm sure you've heard of this word. Self-help gurus everywhere talk about it and athletes in every sport credit their success to it. So what is visualization?

Visualization is seeing with your mind. It is developing pictures inside your head of events, objects, and changes that you want to manifest in your life. It is a powerful way of thinking that allows you to manifest your desires into their physical component.

You can think of visualization as daydreaming; however, it is daydreaming with direction. Unlike a daydream, where your thoughts jump from one scene to another in a random and uncontrolled manner, with visualization, you purposefully direct the scenes in your mind.

In many ways, visualization is a fusion of science and art—a science as it makes use of different scientific methodologies and an art because it involves creativity.

With visualization, you take control of your thoughts, in the form of mental pictures, to create the changes you want and to bring yourself that much closer to the goals you desire. In many cases, it is just a matter of time before they materialize, and, with very intense, vivid and frequent visualizations, often they materialize surprisingly quickly.

CHAPTER 1 – HOW DOES VISUALIZATION WORK?

To understand how visualization works, it helps first to understand how your mind works. Your mind functions on two distinct yet interdependent levels—the conscious and subconscious. The conscious mind is the part that recognizes all the thoughts and feelings that flow through you. When you email a friend, listen to a lecture, phone your mom, or shop for groceries, you are using your conscious mind.

As you concentrate on these thoughts, a large number of processes behind the scenes support you. This is your subconscious at work. You don't logically think through the steps of breathing second to second, and neither do you focus on each trivial task when you are driving a car or walking up a set of stairs. These processes work by themselves, without your observation or concentration. There is a mechanism that maintains and monitors your vital processes, and that mechanism is your subconscious.

For every thought you have in your conscious mind, thousands more occur below the level of consciousness. Thousands of perceptions, assumptions, and decisions are made without your awareness. It is happening all the time, and it is completely hidden from you. When you feel joy or heartbreak, although you recognize the emotion in your conscious mind, it is triggered by your subconscious.

It is important to understand that the conscious and subconscious are not distinct areas of the brain. Rather, they are merely two levels of awareness within your mind and body. You have only one mind, but that mind possesses two distinct functional parts. Each has a different set of objectives to perform, and together, they add up to "YOU."

In addition to maintaining your hidden processes, the subconscious mind also stores information. Everything you hear, see, taste, touch, or smell—along with your dreams, emotions, and behaviors—are dropped into your subconscious, written down in that notebook for later referral. Freud says within your subconscious lies your fears, past failures, habits, and all the things that control your life now.

On top of all this, stored deep within your subconscious are *beliefs*. Beliefs are an extremely important concept. Beliefs control many aspects of yourself, your abilities, your success, and your life. With such a force, let's look more closely at beliefs and how they work.

Beliefs are thoughts you consider to be accurate or real. For example, the thought that *monkeys are animals* is something that you consider to be accurate, as a result, within your subconscious it is a belief. Inside your subconscious, you have thousands and thousands of beliefs about all sorts of things. You may have a belief that *dogs make for great pets* or that *math is a difficult subject*. In addition to dogs and math, you have beliefs about your friends, family, co-workers, your job, hybrid automobiles, democrats, republicans, etc. The list goes on and on.

Above all, you have beliefs about YOURSELF.

You have beliefs about who you are and what you can to do. In addition to the external details such as height, hair color, and gender, your *self* beliefs describe internal aspects of yourself. They describe your strengths and weaknesses, where you stand in the social totem pole, and more importantly, whether you're attractive, intelligent, and important or unattractive, unintelligent and unimportant. In short, your personal beliefs are an awareness of how you understand, interpret, and perceive yourself.

Interestingly, most people think they have the beliefs they have about themselves because that is the way they truly are. If they see themselves as incapable, they think it is because they are, in fact, incapable—and vice versa. This is true to a certain extent; however, to a larger extent, you are the way you are because of your beliefs. Meaning, you are incapable because you believe yourself to be incapable.

You are probably thinking, *how is that possible?*

It is possible because your subconscious is a remarkable power that is one with your mind and body. It shapes and influences, based on your internally held beliefs, your physical and mental abilities as well as your perceptions. If you have negative, self-defeating beliefs like the belief that you are dumb, your subconscious will make you dumb. If you believe that you are unhealthy, your subconscious will create ill health. If you believe the world is a difficult place, your subconscious will do everything in its power to change your thoughts and emotions so you see it as such. As mentioned, the subconscious triggers your thoughts and emotions and it will trigger a mental and emotional state in line with your strongest beliefs.

The opposite is also true. If you hold positive, supportive beliefs like the belief that you can improve your health, your subconscious will work to heal. If you believe you are creative, your subconscious will bring forth new ideas. And if you believe you can succeed and enhance your abilities, your subconscious will guide you in your quest for success. The mental and emotional state it triggers will push you past challenges and limitations and drive you to victory. This is the way your mind is. This is how it works and how it thinks. It acts within the realm of its subconsciously held beliefs.

Many examples confirm this idea. One such example is the placebo effect. The placebo effect is a change in health or behavior of a person not attributable to medication or treatment. Through the placebo effect, patients find themselves healed of illnesses, both mental and physical, just by believing that they are cured. On the opposite end, healthy people become weak and sick simply by being told and accepting they are sick. In these instances, it is not medicine that cures a patient or an illness that makes a patient sick; it is the belief in the person's mind that produces the outcome.

Another example involves the use of lucky charms. Lucky charms are items that people own or carry to bring luck. Examples of popular lucky charms include four-leaf clover, rabbit's foot, horseshoe, and wishbone. Many people attribute their success, good fortune, and livelihood to these items. Though, it's not these objects that bring good fortune. It is the belief these objects create.

Lucky charms do nothing more than create a belief in a person's mind. That belief then connects to an inner strength the person already had and had all along. It is the belief that brings the results, not the object. Unfortunately, if you try to tell these individuals otherwise or take away their so called lucky charm, their flair, talent, dexterity, or whatever benefit they think their supposed charm brought them, flies out the door— with their belief in themselves not far behind.

This is the power of the subconscious to manifest a reality in accordance with your beliefs. Now, it is not to say that a person's inability or ill health are entirely the result of one's beliefs. Though the power that our unconscious beliefs have in our lives is quite interesting. They can literally make or break us as a person.

So where do our beliefs come from? If they are so powerful, the natural question that arises is *how did I come to have the beliefs that I have now?* If beliefs dictate health, wealth, and performance, *why did my mind choose to accept the ones that push these things away from me?*

Beliefs come from many places. For starters, they come from our environment. The environment includes what we learn from parents, peers, teachers, television, radio, books, movies, advertisements, the morning news, etc. Anything that originates from outside ourselves involves this type of programming. Through our environment, we form beliefs about what to do, what to say, how to think, how to act, and how to get along with others around us. Our environment also bestows beliefs about the importance of going to school, the proper way to dress, the importance of hygiene, and as we get older, the correct way to drive and keep a steady job. The environment is one place that we get our beliefs.

Our beliefs also come from ourselves. They come from the thoughts that we say and think to ourselves, and as is the focus of this audio, the mental pictures we replay in our minds. When we replay negative images, like that of failure or insecurity, we form beliefs in accordance with these things. Beliefs that push away the outcomes we desire in life. These beliefs emphasize who we are and our inability to handle the circumstances that come our way. We absorb and reinforce this type of programming without ever realizing that we are doing it.

Going back to the point, the main way visualization works is by modifying your internal pictures to change your beliefs. It replaces negative, limiting images that weaken and take away your personal power with positive, encouraging images—images that form beliefs that give you strength and inner confidence. Through visualization, you change who you are at a core level. It allows you to naturally become the person you want to be and have the success you want to have.

To use an analogy, it helps to think of the mind like a computer. The subconscious is the operating system and hard drive of the mind. The hard drive stores all the files, and the operating system processes all the tasks. When a computer is processing a task, it does so without you having to think about what it is doing. Behind the scenes, however, the computer is sending electronic signals back and forth. You are not conscious of it, but nonetheless, it is silently sending and receiving. The subconscious works the same way. It stores all the files (thoughts, beliefs, emotions) while silently transmitting signals that perform all the tasks (breathing, seeing, hearing).

Then you have the conscious mind, which as stated before is your current state of awareness. Within this analogy, the conscious would be the programmer. Consequently, your beliefs would be the software. To ensure that a computer runs smoothly, the programmer has to install properly functioning software. If he downloads corrupt software, it will limit the performance of the machine. Defective, virus-laden software will not only slow a computer down, but it will drain its energy and cause the computer to perform poorly. The same applies to beliefs. Negative, limiting beliefs not only slow you down, but they sap you of valuable energy while limiting your performance.

To ensure this does not happen to your inner operating system, you, as the programmer of your subconscious, are running only the best, most encouraging software or beliefs. You need to delete the versions that are out of date and infected with viruses of negative belief and replace them with better ones, those that optimize and enhance your performance. Only when you do that can you tap into your inner power to improve yourself, your health, and more importantly, your life.

How might you do that, you ask? With visualization, of course. Visualization is a form of affirmation that harnesses the power of your inner mind to instill positive beliefs that help you perform better, smarter, and faster.

This is not the only way that visualization works to help you. There are many other reasons that make visualization a powerful agent for change. We discuss these in the next chapter.

CHAPTER 2 – OTHER WAYS VISUALIZATION WORKS

In the previous chapter, you learned that visualization helps to manifest change because, like any affirmation, it is the amazing power of thought—not in the form of words, but in pictures—in action. These pictures trigger new beliefs and responses within your subconscious, which guides your decisions and actions.

But beyond triggering beliefs and responses, mental pictures are powerful for many other reasons. For starters, pictures offer you a way to see your beliefs as actual outcomes. Suppose, for example, that you want to use affirmations to become a more confident person. Holding a picture in your mind of what a confident person looks like and how he behaves communicates that idea much more effectively to your subconscious than a verbal description could achieve. No amount of words is going to put that idea into perspective as quickly and easily as a picture. As the old saying goes, *a picture is worth a thousand words*.

Also, mental pictures have a strange power in that your mind instinctively guides you towards the internal pictures you hold inside. Even if you desire something different or better, your mind overrides those desires and moves you in the direction of your mental image. As Emile Coue, the French psychologist who founded the method of healing and self-improvement through affirmations, said, *When the imagination and will power are in conflict, it is always the imagination which wins, without any exception*.

To demonstrate this concept, think back to when you were learning to ride a bike. Remember trying to peddle and balance, making every effort not to fall. Then once you got going, you saw a tree or a rock and became scared that you would run into it. What happened? You ran into it.

Why did that happen, even though that wasn't your intention? That happened because your eyes became fixed on the object you wanted to avoid and your mind physically took control and steered you in the direction of your visual focus. This is the reason skiers and race car drivers are taught never to look at obstacles they want to avoid. Instead, they are told to look in the direction that will maneuver them around those obstacles. Holding that image of where you want to go naturally moves you in that direction.

Since the mind guides you towards the images you hold inside, it makes mental pictures a powerful form of thought. That is because by aligning them with your desires, you more easily move towards it. Even if you have negative thoughts and feelings that say *I can't, that's impossible*, the sound of those voices is muted because your mind looks at the pictures first as its guide.

These are a few reasons why mental pictures are so powerful.

Another reason they are powerful is that to a large part of your unconscious, mental pictures are processed as something real you are seeing and being involved in. That is, to certain parts of the mind, imagining a thing, in a sense, is the same as the thing.

Various scientific studies confirm this fact. In one study, scientists took brain scans of subjects while they were looking at an object, and then again while those subjects developed a mental image of the same object. The brain scans revealed that when a person was told to look at an object, such as someone's face, it activated specific areas of their mind. When that person was told to close their eyes and develop an image of the face, it activated the same areas—as if the two images were processed as one and the same.[1]

That happens because your eyes are really an extension of the brain rather than separate organs. Thus the images you receive from sight travel on many of the same neural pathways as the images you develop mentally. To the parts of the mind that process info

---

[1] *Journal of Cognitive Neuroscience 12:6, pp. 1013–1023*

from these neural pathways, the images seem to be one and the same.

You don't need science to verify this scenario. You can experience it for yourself. Imagine a slice of lemon—beautiful, yellow with citrus texture, and dripping with juice. Now imagine putting it on your tongue. Let it sit there. Feel the lemony, tangy taste of that lemon as it rests there. Notice how your mouth starts to water and you're taken aback by its sourness?

How did that happen? There was no lemon sitting on your tongue. It was just your imagination. Although a smaller part of you knows the lemon is imagined, a bigger part of your unconscious experiences it as real. That's why your mouth waters, as it is right now.

We can demonstrate this concept with any number of images. Imagine biting into a cotton ball or imagine a cockroach crawling on your arm. How do these things make you feel? They likely make you cringe as if they are really happening.

You are probably wondering what makes the ability of your unconscious to process mental images as real so powerful? It's powerful for two reasons. First, it enhances your mind's ability to create beliefs. Since images are perceived as real, they are stored and remembered within your subconscious as something real. Real experiences, even if only seemingly real, integrate into beliefs more readily.

Second, it allows you to use mental images, and hence visualization, in ways that go beyond simply changing beliefs. As you will learn in the subsequent chapters, you can use visualization in many ways. You can use it, in the form of mental practice, to improve any number of physical and mental skills. You can also use it, in the form of guided imagery, to induce relaxation and control physical processes of the mind and body not normally under your conscious control. These are few of the many benefits.

As you can see, there is a lot of power in your mental pictures, and visualization helps you tap into that power. It can help you take your ability to perform and achieve to exceptional levels. Best of all, it's a resource each and every person possesses. In the next chapter, you will learn how to put this resource to work for you in different areas of your life.

CHAPTER 3 – THE ART & SCIENCE OF VISUALIZATION

Due to the intrinsic nature of images, visualizations can be done in a variety of ways. In fact, the variations are infinite. Though, whichever variation you use, the technique is basically the same. You develop an image in your mind of the outcomes you desire.

In this program, we break down the infinite variations of visualization into four categories. Each category has its own strengths that deal with the specific outcomes you desire.

They are:

• Outcome/Object Visualization

• Self-Image

• Mental Rehearsal

• Guided Imagery

We discuss each variation in detail in the following pages.

Outcome/Object Visualization

In this visualization, you visualize an object or outcome you desire. For example, if you desire to own your own home, you visualize in detail the type of home you want to own and picture yourself owning it. If you desire a particular outcome, like acing a history test, you picture yourself correctly answering all the questions and receiving an "A" mark on the exam.

You are probably wondering how visualizing something is going to magically get you what you want. I never said that your desires come to pass magically, although sometimes it seems to happen that way.

They come to pass for the reasons we discussed earlier. Visualizations create beliefs of attainability. They also create a clear destination in your mind of the outcome you want. More importantly, they change the inner pictures within your mind so that you are no longer guided by pictures of frustration and difficulty. When you have all these features working together, you increase your chances of achieving the things you want in life–more quickly and easily.

Also, as people, many of the thoughts we have about success are in relation to why we can't have it. In our minds, we have analyzed all the reasons why things can't work, aren't going to work, or will never work. Whether or not the reasons are true, they have a way of becoming true. That's because our expectations of failure, in a sense, guide us to it. Negative expectations create negative attitudes that become a self-fulfilling prophecy. And you wonder why you move towards the things you don't want.

When you visualize, you put the negative expectations to the side and picture what it is that you truly want. This gives your unconscious a clear objective, one that focuses on solutions rather than problems. It sees a new destination and looks for the easiest path to get there. Even if the path doesn't show up consciously, your unconscious sees and guides you along it, creating the impression that the desire manifested magically.

Joseph Murphy illustrates this in his classic best seller, *The Power of Your Subconscious Mind*. In one of the chapters, he talks about a young girl in a complicated lawsuit. The lawsuit created an expectation of failure, loss, bankruptcy, and poverty in this person. Joseph Murphy suggested that she change these expectations with positive imagery. At his suggestion,

> *She began to dramatize as vividly as possible her lawyer having an animated discussion with her regarding the outcome. She would ask him questions, and he would answer her appropriately. [She imagined] he would say to her over and over again, "There has been a perfect, harmonious solution. The case has been settled out of court." At the end of a few*

weeks her attorney called her and confirmed objectively what she had been imagining . . . .

This illustrates how visualization brought a positive outcome. Had the young woman not visualized, there is a chance the legal matter would have turned out well. However, more than likely, negative expectations would have gotten in the way. Her fears and apprehensions would have caused her to procrastinate on important tasks. Her anxiety would have caused her to lose focus on critical issues. If the frightened girl had to stand in front of a judge or jury, her pessimistic attitude could very well have made her look suspicious and untrustworthy. Worse, if her negative outlook were strong enough, she might have given up, feeling that there was no use in trying. Her expectations would have created a self-fulfilling prophecy of the outcome she feared.

Instead, her mental pictures overrode all of that. Her images kept her calm, even though a positive outcome seemed impossible. They gave her focus so she could pay attention to issues without distractions. More importantly, the pictures presented a vision of an end goal, one she set her eyes on and achieved.

Now that you recognize the benefits of outcome visualization, use the following exercise to direct you through the process.

Outcome/Object Exercise

The key factor to using this exercise properly is to have a goal in mind. Again, your goal can be an object or outcome. When figuring out this goal, be as specific as possible. The more specific, the better. For example, instead of simply saying you want a new car, specify the type of car that you want. Narrow in on the make, the model, the color, etc. If you are looking for a relationship, figure out the type of relationship for which you are seeking. If you want prosperity, change your *I want to be rich* wish to *I want a specific dollar amount in the bank*.

Why the need to be specific? Vague desires create ambiguity. Ambiguity overwhelms your mind with too many decisions and *what if* scenarios. For example, when you say you want a relationship, a relationship can mean a lot of things. Do you want a relationship with a man or a woman? Do you want that relationship to be a friendship or something more intimate? If it is intimacy, what kind of intimacy are you looking for and with what kind of person? Should that person be old or young, mature or fun, serious or lighthearted? The possibilities are endless.

With so many possibilities, it can be too much for your mind to work through. As a result, many times it won't. Instead, your mind will choose the easiest option, one that may not lead you to your intended desire. Therefore, make sure to specify that desire. Figure out precisely what you want and how you want it to look. Don't assume your unconscious will automatically know every aspect of your conscious needs.

Now that you understand the importance of being specific, take a few moments to think about some goals, dreams, and wishes for your life. Once you have some outcomes in mind, sit or lie down in a comfortable position. Straighten your back and let your arms and legs reach their natural positions. Take a deep breath and hold it for 5-10 seconds. While slowly exhaling, mentally say *relax* and release the tension from every part of your body.

First, close your eyes and turn your attention inwards. Slowly clear your mind of all thoughts and focus on the object or situation you desire. Is it a car, an expensive piece of jewelry, a new job? Whatever it is, *see* it in front of you. Notice every aspect of the object or outcome.

Next, see yourself in possession of it. If it's jewelry or clothing, see yourself wearing it. If it's a car or house, see yourself inside enjoying it. If it's a new promotion, see yourself living it—at the office making important decisions.

Furnish the image with as much detail as possible. If you are visualizing graduation day, is it inside or outside? If it is outside, what is the weather like? Is your family there with you? If they are, picture them in the audience feeling proud of your accomplishment. If you are imagining your dream car, what is the interior like? Picture all the options, the leather, the trimming, even the speedometer. Are you on the open road? If so, see the scenery race by while driving.

Most importantly, feel the feelings associated with attaining your outcome. When you acquire or achieve something, a feeling arises. That feeling can be excitement, triumph, or even relief because you now have what you have always wanted. Evoke that feeling. Get excited, feel your heart race, and feel the enthusiasm you now have as a result of attaining this desire. As you will learn in a subsequent chapter, the emotional response to an image is very important, so get your feelings involved.

During the process, if you have negative thoughts or feelings come up telling you that your mental picture is unrealistic, too difficult to attain, or too much of a day dream, do your best to ignore them for the time being. Don't worry about *how* you are going to afford the new car or the new house. Don't bother with the details at this point. Your job is only to visualize your success completely and program your unconscious.

Now, slowly allow yourself to return to the present moment. Open your eyes and be aware of your surroundings. Affirm in your mind that the object or job belongs to you and that you will soon be getting it in your hand.

Do this exercise twice daily for all of your goals, once in the morning when you wake up, and once at night, just before you go to bed.

Self-Image Visualization

This next technique is similar to object visualization, except the object of the visualization is you. It is a great way to improve the way you want to look, act, and feel. For example, if you are trying to lose weight, in addition to a diet and exercise regimen, you imagine yourself as the newer and slimmer you. If you want to break out of shyness or if you want to eliminate nervous ticks, you picture the new you with the qualities you want.

The same principles that govern outcome visualization apply here—they change beliefs, create a clear target, and replace faulty images and expectations in your mind.

A big proponent of this technique, and visualization as a whole, is Arnold Schwarzenegger. Yes, I'm talking about the former governor of California. As you know, before he became governor, he was a movie icon starring in blockbusters such as *The Terminator* and *Kindergarten Cop*. Though, before he was a screen legend, he was a seven-time Mr. Universe champion.

In September, 2005, Arnold Schwarzenegger gave a commencement speech to the students at his alma mater in Santa Monica College. In the speech, he advocated the value of using visualization in their lives.

He said, *I can't over-emphasize how important it is to see your success. Fill your head with it.*

The Terminator went on further to say that his seven-time Mr. Universe physique was no mere accident. He mentally sculpted his body just as much as he physically sculpted it. He stated:

> *I saw myself as Mr. Universe. I saw what the body would look like . . . . I had a clear vision of the goal. Then it was just a matter of doing the exercises, pumping all the iron, bit by bit, slowly and steadily, year after year—until I got to take a shot at it—and won.*

His speech is very motivating and worth reading.

If you don't know much about Arnold's physique, at one point, many considered it the most perfect representation of a developed male body—more perfect than anyone in history. If he attributes so much of this success to visualization, think how much it can help you. This is not to say that you have to set self-image goals to become Mr. Universe. Whatever your goals are, though, start in your mind first, and soon they will come to pass in your life.

What are you waiting for? Start right now.

Again, get into a comfortable position, close your eyes, and let go. Take a deep breath and hold it for 5-10 seconds. Exhale slowly and mentally say *relax*. Release any physical, emotional, or mental tension as you exhale.

Now turn your attention inward. Imagine that you are standing in front of a mirror. The mirror is a full body mirror, so you can see yourself from head to toe. Look at your reflection in it. See the reflection not as you are, though, but as you'd like to be.

Notice your physique. How does it look? If you want to lose weight, picture yourself fit and thin. If your goal is to gain muscle, picture yourself muscular and strong. Picture each part of the body—calves, thighs, butt, stomach, back, chest, arms, and shoulders—as you'd like it to be. If you have love handles you'd like to get rid of, imagine yourself without them. If you'd like washboard abs, place them in your image. You have a healthy, attractive physique.

Look at your posture. How are you standing? If you want to improve your posture, do so here. Good posture means standing straight with your head up and chin level to the ground. Your shoulders should be pulled down and slightly back with your weight distributed evenly between both feet. Your body should not be rigid nor tense, but relaxed. Adjust the posture in your reflection to fit this description. If there are special aspects of your posture you'd like to correct, fine-tune them accordingly. Your posture is strong and confident.

What about your expression? Are you tense and nervous? Do you fidget, stutter, twitch, or have jerky movements? If so, remove these features from the reflection. Are there other characteristics of your appearance that you dislike, maybe stress and tired eyes, rigid disposition, or a worry demeanor? Strip off these peculiarities and make your reflection look calm, open, and inviting. You look pleasing and feel pleasant.

Now, rotate the reflection in the mirror as if it is revolving on a turntable. See all sides of the image standing tall and attractive. Rotate the image a few times so your unconscious clearly grasps all parts of it.

Next, take that ideal image and see it walking. It is walking as though it belongs. See it talking. It is talking with confidence that people are interested in what it is saying. Put the image in a stressful scenario and see it maintain composure. It handles everything with ease. Feel the poise and the pride that this mental image possesses. You like what you see.

Now that you have an ideal image, see it come out of the mirror. However, see not just one image come out, but thousands. Thousands of the new you are everywhere. They are in front of you and behind you. They are close to you and far off in the distance. They are even in your past, present, and future. They are everywhere.

Now see them walking through you. As they do, their posture, demeanor, energy, confidence, beliefs and everything you imagined in them transfer to you.

Now start walking. As you walk, you go through them. The more you go through, the more like them you become.   Your body is changing, your posture is changing, and your expressions are changing. The way you look, act, and feel are all changing to make you more like the ideal image.   You feel strong and poised, capable, positive, ready for action.

Stay in this image for a moment. When you are ready, you can come back.

Using visualization this way allows you to change your self-image. You replace the old with the new, and the new are like instructions to your subconscious of the person you want to become. All this makes it easier to move toward the better you—the you of your dreams.

With this exercise, you do not have to work on all the areas we went through here—physique, posture, expression, confidence—at one time. You can isolate one or two of the areas. That is, if your main concern is to lose weight, then simply direct your attention to the part of the visualization that addresses the physique you desire.   If you simply want to remove unwanted nervousness, center your image on eliminating that. Feel free to personalize this exercise to the specific change you crave.

Mental Practice

On any given Sunday during the summer, you will inevitably find Tiger Woods contending for yet another PGA trophy. Watch carefully and you will notice that before every shot, Tiger goes through a routine of taking practice swings and visualizing how the ball will fly. He visualizes the perfect shot and feels his body, arms and hands executing that shot. He can see the trajectory of the ball, whether it curves left or right, where it will land, and whether it will spin back or stop on a dime. Tiger has visualization down to such a science that by the time he takes the actual shot, it's just another repetition of the perfect swings he's already made.

This description of Tiger Woods' routine you just read is a visualization technique called mental practice. Mental practice is rehearsing a skill you want to learn or improve in the mind instead of actual practice. Unlike outcome and self-model visualizations, where you picture the end result of your desire, with this technique, you paint the entire process of rehearsing a task.

As mentioned earlier, you can use visualization for different types of self-improvement, and this is one of them. Athletes in almost every field routinely apply mental rehearsal to develop their skills and to help them perform on the field. The following is a small list of thousands of professional and Olympic athletes who have incorporated visualization, specifically mental practice, into their routine.

• Trent Dimas – Gymnastics – Olympic Gold Medalist
• Laura Wilkinson – High Dive – Olympic Gold Medalist
• Jackie Joyner-Kersee – Track – Olympic Gold Medalist
• Michael Johnson – Track – Olympic Gold Medalist
• Dick Fosbury – High Jump – Olympic Gold Medalist and creator of the Fosbury Flop
• Tiger Woods – Golf – Four PGA Championships
• Jack Nicklaus – Golf – Five PGA Championships

As you see, world-class athletes and peak performers in almost every field rely on this technique to give them the edge they need to win. They are masters of mental simulation. Since top athletes in every field attest to the positive effects of visualization, especially in the form of mental practice, imagine the improvements it can bring in your life. In essence, if you are not applying this skill, you don't truly desire improvement.

Mental practice is effective for many reasons. First, mental practice in many ways is real practice. Each time you physically practice an action, you engrave neural patterns, similar to small tracks, in the brain. Many scientific studies show that mentally practicing an activity creates the same neural patterns as if you physically performed the action. By rehearsing performance in your mind, essentially you create neural patterns that help you manifest performance in real life.

Furthermore, mental practice helps you rehearse tasks using proper techniques. When you practice physically, there is a tendency to do it incorrectly. This ingrains improper habits into your subconscious. However, with mental practice, you see yourself do it right, whether it's the perfect golf swing or the perfect basketball shot. You observe the action and continually adjust the image until you have the proper mechanics down pat. Because many actions in actual practice occur too fast to process, with mental practice, you can slow down the speed of, change the angle, or even rewind the image to refine every aspect of the perfect routine. Since the practice is real to the mind, you enhance execution in real life.

Lastly, mental practice has a unique way of helping you cope with fears and apprehensions that come from high pressure situations. When doing a routine under pressure, say trying to hit the game-winning shot at the buzzer, negative thoughts and anxiety have a tendency to seep in. You might start thinking *the game is on the line, I can't screw this up*. These thoughts have a way of distracting you and sabotaging your performance.

Mental practice helps you cope by allowing you to rehearse situations under pressure. Since the emotional effect of a mental image is real, you can recreate pressure situations in your mind to trigger many of the same thoughts and fears the actual experience would trigger. Then you would practice how you would carry yourself in the face of those thoughts and fears. You would mentally see yourself acting calmly and decisively. You would see yourself make the shot, hit the home run, or run for the touchdown to win the game, series, or championship. By visualizing this way, you practice in the face of your fears and apprehensions. Also, you ingrain images of the outcome you desire—making the shot or hitting the home run. In the actual situation, it is these images that your mind will lead with to give you the winning outcome.

These are some of the many reasons mental practice improves your performance to deliver the positive results. Now, even if you don't aspire to be a star athlete, you can still apply this technique in your life. As mentioned earlier, you can use this tool to improve any number of physical and mental skills. You might use it to improve a sales presentation, a job interview, a dance routine, or anything else that involves, well, practice.

Mental Practice Exercise

Once again, take a couple of deep breaths and let your body unwind. Loosen your muscles and exhale deeply. Close your eyes and imagine yourself confident, strong, without an inkling of doubt in your mind and body (if you have inklings of doubt, for the exercise, put them to the side for the moment).

Now think about a skill or ability you'd like to perform to perfection. See you in your mind performing the activity. If it's an athletic routine like a baseball swing or football throw, see yourself performing it with precision. First pay close attention to your balance and posture. Are your arms and feet in the right place? Are you looking in the right direction? Are you properly aligned? If not, fix these things in your image. Rotate and change the angle of the image to make sure all parts of your body are lined up correctly.

Next, see the flawless execution of the routine. If you are practicing a football throw, see yourself cast the ball in the direction you intend. Visualize all parts of your body moving in sync and see the grace in your action. Slow down the mental movie and focus on correctly initiating each of the parts of your body to create the proper movements. Feel your muscles moving together like a well-oiled machine, neither tiring nor straining.

Now, look down, back up, where are you? You are at the game. The season is on the line, the clock is winding down, you are behind by one possession, and the last play is in your hands. The fans are cheering and screaming. The coach is yelling in the distance. Your see your opponent in front determined to stop you. The pressure and tension are building.

Instead of the letting the pressure affect you, picture yourself calm and in control. Nothing in this scenario is distracting you or getting in the way of your decision making. You see the situation, you see the opponent, you are well aware of their movements and patterns. You see an opening. You act quickly and decisively. You've made the game winning play. The fans are cheering.

If you are rehearsing an interview, sales presentation, or speech, picture yourself in front of your audience. See yourself addressing them calm and confidently. Watch yourself speaking. As you speak, hear the knowing in your voice and feel the power of your thoughts washing over your audience. If nervousness and tension arise, see yourself remain cool in the face of these emotions. The feelings are there, but they don't affect you or throw you off balance. Everything is running smoothly from start to finish.

In addition, pay attention to your words. If there are glitches in your argument, work them out. As the audience or interviewer raises difficult questions and objections, picture yourself handling them with ease. Their objections don't faze you in the slightest bit. In fact, you're glad they raised them, because now you can display how much you know and how prepared you are. Mentally run through the arguments that will tactfully address their concerns.

Run through the mental sequence a few times. Notice those areas that make you feel tense and uneasy. These are signs of sticking points. In most cases, they are weaknesses that require extra attention. Focus additional time and effort in working out and developing these areas.

After you've gone through the routine a few times, imagine the end result that you desire. If you are practicing an athletic routine to win in competition, see yourself winning. If you are rehearsing an interview to land a prestigious job, see the interviewer offer you the position—at the salary level you desire. Never leave this step out—always picture the end result.

When you feel content with your rehearsal, slowly bring yourself back to the present moment and open your eyes.

Do this exercise often. Use it in all areas of your life. Whether you are an athlete or an aspiring executive, dancer or musician, or if you do anything that requires coordination, skill, and speed, mental practice can help you perfect your moves.

Note: Mental practice is not a substitute for real practice. Although this technique is an indispensable tool for personal growth, it cannot take the place of actual practice. Nevertheless, when combined, mental practice will enhance your skills above and beyond physical practice alone.

Guided Imagery/Meditation

Before moving forward, let's take a short break. You've read a lot and absorbed a ton of information, so a relaxing diversion is in order.

For this break, close your eyes and imagine yourself walking along a white sandy beach at daybreak. The sun is pleasantly warm, and you can feel its rays caressing your skin. Overhead, the clear blue sky looks warm and peaceful with lazy tufts of clouds sailing by.

Now, turn your attention to the sounds around you. You can hear the gentle lapping of water and the faint call of birds. The breeze is gently rustling the leaves, allowing you to hear the sound of coconut palms swaying in the light wind. Notice the scent in the air. It's a hint of summer breeze.

Allow your mind to dwell in this place for a little while longer. Take a few deep breaths and explore a bit. When you are ready to return, slowly bring your attention back to this program. Know that you can go back to this haven whenever you wish.

This escape you just experienced is an example of a visualization technique called guided imagery. Guided imagery is a gentle but powerful technique that creates an experience in the mind. It uses metaphors, scene-telling, fantasy, and exploration to create various types of imagery. You may imagine yourself at the beach, in the clouds, or in a safe and ideal environment.

Guided imagery is a great mind-body intervention used to induce relaxation, counteract stress, and improve your mood. Since images are real to the mind, they influence many processes of the body that are normally not under your conscious control. This includes breathing, heart rate, blood pressure, metabolism, and even immune system function.

A calming image of a walk along the beach with the tender rays from the sun warming your body helps trigger relaxation. If you notice, it has an immediate effect. You breathe slower, and the tension in your head and muscles seems to melt away. When done properly, it has the effect of shutting off the automatic thoughts that the mind runs almost non-stop and allows you to take a mini-vacation.

Guided Imagery has also been found to promote healing, both mentally and physically. In the imagery you see cancer tumors shrinking or warts disappearing, and you can even imagine yourself surrounded by healing energy or a white cleansing light filling you inside and dissolving negativity. It is a safe complement or alternative to medical intervention which is finding scientific acceptance.

Over 200 research studies in the past 30 years have explored the role of mind-body techniques in helping prepare people for surgical and medical procedures and helping them recover more rapidly. These studies have shown that guided imagery may significantly reduce stress and anxiety before and after surgical and medical procedures. In addition, guided imagery has been proven to:

• *Dramatically decrease pain and the need for pain medication*

• *Decrease side effects and complications of medical procedures*

• *Reduce recovery time and shorten hospital stays*

• *Enhance sleep*

• *Strengthen the immune system and enhance the ability to heal*

• *Increase self-confidence and self-control*

In addition to helping patients cope during a medical or surgical procedure, guided imagery can help patients undergoing chemotherapy, dialysis, in vitro fertilization, or other treatment procedures[2]

The power of visualization to influence your body is quite remarkable. The term *mind over matter* applies to all aspects of your life, but nowhere is it more noticeable than in sessions of guided imagery, where a person instantly feels the effect of what his or her mind sees.

The following is a great exercise with which to get started. It takes many of the benefits of guided imagery and all the possible ways to do them and puts them into a single exercise. This way you can come back to it often and use it to handle all your healing and relaxation needs.

Guided Imagery Exercise

Sit or lie down comfortably. Loosen any restrictive clothing and relax. Take a deep breath and hold it for a few seconds. As you exhale, imagine all worries and stress flowing out. Focus your attention on different parts of the body and release the tension in every group of muscles. Once your body is relaxed, turn your attention to your breathing. With each breath, feel your breathing become more and more easy.

In your mind, see yourself standing in front of a mysterious cave. As you approach the entrance of the cave, you notice that inside, it is well-lit. As you get

[2]http://www.clevelandclinic.org/health/health-info/docs/3900/3920.asp?index=12512

closer, you can see darts of colorful light dancing on the stones. Now walking into the cave, you see the most amazing sight. There, on the ground and on the rocks, you see hundreds of crystal balls. These crystal balls are different in color, and each one is pulsing with energy and radiating brightly.

You notice that each orb carries a certain power within it. For instance, the red orb gives confidence. The white supplies health. The yellow bestows peace while the pink grants self-esteem.

Determine the strength you are seeking for this session. Are you looking to relax? Do you want to overcome an illness? Are you searching for inner peace? Locate the ball with the strength or healing you seek. If you are unsure of what you are seeking, allow your instincts to guide you. Look at the different orbs and pick the one that seems to be calling out to you for this session. Let your intuition lead you to the strength you need.

Once you've identified the orb, pick it up. Notice its energy pulsating in your hands. It has a kind, soothing feeling. Now, see the energy spreading from the orb through every cell of your body. First it fills your hands. Then it moves up your arms. Next, it spreads to your chest and shoulders. Afterwards, it moves up to your head and down to your feet, encapsulating every part of your being. You are shining with an intense, colorful glow.

As the color of the energy spreads, feel its power traveling through you. The vigor and force of the energy inside you dissolves away negativity. As the negativity melts away, the energy transfers the strength and healing you desire.

If you desire health, imagine the orb's energy healing you. See the colorful energy working to treat your precise ailment. If you are sick, picture the curing light killing the bacteria, virus, or cancer cells causing the ill health. If you are injured, imagine the healing color mending your wound. If your problems stem from a malfunctioning organ, such as the heart or liver, see the shining, energetic light restoring the organ to a proper functioning state. Your heart is beating strongly. Your lungs are expanding resiliently. The healing power of the orb is eliminating pain and bringing you to a firm, healthy state.

If you desire inner peace, imagine the energy washing way your personal turmoil. The reassuring light removes your stress, anxiety, and insecurities. It fills you with comfort and assurance. You feel tranquil and at peace.

Relax in this experience. Feel the healing, confidence, and relaxation the energy transfers to you. Once you're ready, open your eyes and slowly come back to the present moment. Feel the change in your state of mind and body. Notice how the new you feels re-charged, more energetic, healthier and enthusiastic.

Whenever you need to relax, renew, recharge, heal, overcome difficulty, etc., do this exercise. Simply choose a strength that you desire and go to your cave and find the orb that will fill you with it. Rest assured that the cave will always have an orb to give you what you need, helping you in all ways, and always.

These are some of the different types of visualizations—outcome/object, self-image, mental practice, and guided imagery—you can do. As mentioned earlier, although the methods vary, the technique is essentially the same. You figure out what you want, decide how you want the outcome to look, and then picture it in your mind's eye.

It is not a stretch of the imagination to say that you likely have dozens upon dozens of things you want to have and achieve in life. Nonetheless, don't attempt to visualize everything at once. Start off with a few items, objectives that are easy, or won't take a long time to attain. This way you won't overwhelm yourself or your mind in the beginning. It's like physical exercise. You don't begin working out by running a marathon. You have to train and build up your skill. The same applies with visualization.

Once you become accustomed to visualizing and finding the sequence that is right for you, you can expand your list and start including more and bigger goals. You may even be able to practice your visualization outside of a relaxed state. So remember, whatever your goals, visualize them first—all worthwhile achievements begin in the mind.

CHAPTER 4 – VISUALIZATION GUIDELINES

So far you have learned not only the importance of visualizing, but also the different ways you can apply visualization in your life. Just as with any skill, there are guidelines you need to follow to ensure your visualizations are effective. The guidelines are:

• Picture the Details

• Involve Your Senses

• Visualize from Both View Points

• Visualize with Belief

• Visualize with Emotion

• Visualize in a Relaxed State

• Visualize Often

We go over each of these guidelines in this chapter.

Picture the Details

When you form the visual image in your mind, see the details. Detail means include in the image as many subtle elements and fine points as possible. For example, if it is a car that you want, see the color of the exterior. Picture the interior. What does the speedometer look like? If you are visualizing a person, notice his or her clothes. Is he or she standing with a good posture or stoop-shouldered? Look at the person's eye color; see the wrinkles, dimples, and his or her smile. If it is a big promotion, see yourself in your new office. Mentally furnish it with your personal effects. See the name plate on your new desk with your name on it.

Picturing the detail is important because your external reality is detailed. If you look around, you will see the room, office, or coffee shop you are in fitted with tables, chairs, pictures of various types, walls of various colors, and floors with various patterns. There are files spread out and books lying around. Although you may not pick up on these nuances, your subconscious does. Therefore, if you want your inner images to hold up within your subconscious, you have to provide detail in accordance with your outer reality. The more realistic you make the image, the more your subconscious will buy into it.

Involve Your Senses

Visualization is something you do with your mind, not your eyes alone, so don't limit yourself to just visual imagery. When you visualize, incorporate your other senses as well, such as sound, smell, and even taste. Hear the audience cheering when you deliver the perfect speech. Smell the leather interior of your dream car. Taste the cookies you baked in your new home. Observe all the senses in that image.

Involving your senses is important for the same reason as adding detail. It makes your image more realistic, giving it more credibility within your unconscious. Don't get stuck on the visual aspect of visualization. Visions in the mind are not limited to seeing. Often, the most important aspects are not visual at all.

Visualize from Both View Points

Visualization can be done from two points of view. You can see yourself in the visualization, like watching a video screen, or you can recreate a sequence from within yourself, as if you are in the screen. When you visualize, it is important to run the scene from both of these view points.

To illustrate, say you want to use visualization to practice a speech in your mind. First, you picture yourself in the distance, as if you are observing the image from the audience. You see yourself standing behind the podium calm and relaxed, ready and prepared. From this viewpoint, you imagine going through the entire routine, delivering the speech with unwavering finesse. Here, you are not in the image. You are outside looking in, like watching an actor in a movie, except the actor is you.

Then you take that image you created of the perfect you and put yourself inside it. Here, you are no longer viewing yourself from afar; rather, you are experiencing the image. You are in front of the audience with your notes in hand. From this place, you go through the routine just as you pictured earlier. Notice how from this angle you might be more tense and apprehensive. That's because from this viewpoint, you experience the situation as you would in real life. As the feelings of tension and apprehension arise, see yourself acting in spite of them. Run through the routine as you imagined yourself before—relaxed, ready, and composed.

This is what we mean by points of view. One is in the 3rd person, where you watch yourself in the distance. The other is in the 1st person, where you are inside yourself. Each point offers an experience the other cannot. In the 3rd person, you can see your body, movements, and expressions. In the 1st person, you are more aware of your inner thoughts and feelings. To get a fuller experience from your visualization exercise, run the sequence from both points. You don't have to do both viewpoints in one sitting, but make sure to change up your visualization regularly.

Beliefs

As you have learned, beliefs are powerful. They influence your decisions, actions, and reality. As a result, when you visualize, visualize with belief. Believe that what you are visualizing is attainable, even though you don't yet see *how* it can be. You will necessarily be stretching your limits because you don't currently have the thing you are imagining. Nonetheless, believe that it is possible and possible for you.

The highest level of belief is acceptance. You just know that it will happen. Feelings of acceptance are difficult to conceive, especially in the beginning. Nonetheless, realize that the mere fact that you are going through the visualization process is an expression of your positive acceptance. If in the slightest bit you didn't accept this technique to work or bring results, you would not be doing it. Don't waste time wondering whether you have the right degree of acceptance—just imagine that you do. This is visualization, right? So accept it will happen.

Emotions

Emotions play a critical role in our lives. That is because as humans we are in a constant flux of emotions. When we wake up in the morning, we feel cranky. When there is a deadline to meet, we feel rushed. When we have to take an exam or give a presentation, we feel stressed. When things don't go our way, we feel anger or disappointment. When we anticipate a positive outcome, we feel excitement. When the unexpected happens, we feel surprise. When something dreadful happens, we feel fear. When something good happens, we feel happy. When we are not experiencing any of these events, we may feel either peace or restlessness because we expect to be in some sort of emotive state. No matter who the person and what the situation or outcome, we are always in a feeling state.

Not only are we always in a constant flux of emotions, but our emotions influence how we respond to situations or outcomes. If we feel anxiety, it may cause us to over react. If we feel hopeless, it may prevent us from acting at all. Since we are always in an emotional state and those emotions drive our decisions and actions, you want to make sure to visualize with positive emotion. As you picture the desired result in your mind and convince yourself of the outcome's possibility, feel the quiet contentment, breathless excitement, or the loads of fun. Feel the joy of it happening and coming in to being. Emotions make the image more real, adding acceptance and triggering productive decisions and actions.

Relaxed State

Many people find that being in a relaxed state is helpful, perhaps even essential for the process. Numerous studies show that your unconscious is more receptive to suggestions when relaxed. In a calm state, your unconscious does not resist or argue with the images as much. It more willingly accepts and goes along with the illustrations you are presenting. This allows you to ingrain them into beliefs more readily.

Also, being relaxed makes the process of visualizing easier. Visualizing can be a challenge, especially in the beginning. As you try to form a picture, your active and out-of-control mind may battle with you. It may make it difficult to produce a concrete picture, or it will throw things into the image that you don't want, or it will make it difficult for you to hold the image long enough to make out the important details.

Often, the image may create feelings of anxiety and tension because it is not in line with your internal beliefs and habits. If the anxiety and tension are strong enough, your mind will jump to a completely unrelated thought just so it can avoid the pain the picture brings. In these instances, you will find yourself three to five to ten minutes later on another thought and wondering how you got there, only to realize you were initially trying to visualize.

By relaxing your mind and body, you eliminate these distractions and disruptions. This helps you to mold an image exactly as you want while enjoying the process. What's more, for certain types of visualization, relaxation supplements the technique. For exercises like guided imagery, much of the healing, stress reduction, and pain relief occur as a direct result of relaxing. It is a fundamental ingredient in the visualization recipe.

To get into a relaxed state, you can use any of the relaxation exercises presented in the previous chapter. Each one will help you quiet the conscious and subconscious so there is less resistance to the image. If you want, you can use relaxation scripts from other sources like books and CDs as well. The internet is filled with relaxation scripts which may prove to be more effective for you. Use whatever helps you calm down and ease into the visualization process.

Visualize Often

The last and the most important point is to visualize your goals often. It is important to apply visualization consistently until you achieve the desired result. Doing the exercise once or twice or sporadically here and there is not likely to give you the outcome you desire. It can happen, but is not as probable.

This is not a hard-and-fast rule, but a good routine is to visualize each goal twice daily. We recommend once in the morning before getting out of bed and once in the evening before you fall asleep. It helps to do this for at least 30 days or until you achieve or see the results you desire.

Keep in mind that different visualizations will transpire at different times and in different ways. Some, like practicing for an interview or presentation, you will achieve rather quickly, so you will not need to act on them for long periods of time. Others, like losing weight or improving health, may take time to transpire and so will require that you stick with them until you start seeing results. Thus, stay with your goals and visualize them often.

These are the guidelines to keep in mind when you visualize. Make sure to notice the details, involve your senses, see the image from both view points, visualize with belief, emotions, and in a relaxed state, and more importantly, do it often. Although it seems like a lot of stuff to remember and a bit overwhelming to do, it is not. Once you get the hang of it, you will be able to do it without thinking twice.

CONCLUSION

Some of you may dismiss visualization, claiming that you are not a visual person. That's just your unconscious making excuses. The truth is that everyone has some ability to visualize. It would be difficult to get dressed in the morning if you couldn't conjure up a mental image of what to wear, what colors go with what, and how you will look at the office. That is, even something as simple as getting dressed in the morning requires some sort of visualization.

While most people use visualization unconsciously for these day-to-day tasks, they do not use visualization consciously to improve the more significant aspects of their lives. Instead, most people hold pictures of limitation and difficulty, which causes them to maintain a limiting mind set. If you want to improve the pictures in your life, you must first improve the pictures in your mind.

With that said, don't be discouraged if you have difficulty manipulating images or are unable to visualize clearly. Visualization is a skill that takes practice, and just as with any skill, with consistent effort, your visualization skills will improve. Trust yourself and be patient. As your visualization skills improve, so will the quality of life you lead.

* * *

I see a lot of people wanting to do and have more in their lives. Unfortunately, because of their unconscious programming and mindset, they experience difficulty at every turn. This program was produced to help people overcome their limitations to more easily attract those things they desire.

As you may have gathered, Visualization isn't complicated. It's simply a matter of picturing in your mind's eye the improvements and changes you'd like to manifest.

It's for this reason the audio was kept concise. If you notice, it lacks any unnecessary and superfluous conversations and includes only the essential points for using and succeeding with the technique. This way, instead of wasting time reading about visualization, you can start using it to immediately improve your life.

Hopefully you felt that this program provided that. If you did, please leave a positive review of it where you made the purchase. It will motivate others to learn about visualization and to put it to use.

Lastly, visualization goes hand in hand with two other very important concepts: Goal Setting and Self-Talk. If you want to take your ability to succeed to the next level, consider also listening to:

Goal Setting: Discover What You Want in Life and Achieve it Faster than You Think Possible – Second Edition by Kam Knight

Self-Talk Your Way to Success by Kam Knight

Printed in Great Britain
by Amazon